Expressions
From
Within

W. T. Cole

WTC Publishing ◆ Memphis

Expressions From Within

WTC Publishing
Memphis, Tennessee

Production
Virtual Marketing & Publishing
Memphis, Tennessee

ISBN: 978-0-9789467-0-8

Ronna Zinn – Editing, Layout, Cover Design
June Santonastasi - Final Cover Art

Fourth Edition
Printed in the U.S.A.

Prelude-Dedication

This book is an expression of various thoughts and feelings which I have experienced for years. I dedicate this compilation of poems to my mother, Mary Elizabeth Crite, my late father, James E. Cole, my beautiful wife, Angela Cole, my talented kids, Eurika, Justin, Auriel, Alexis, Terrence, Christina, Alex and Aiden. You all are my pride and joy. I thank God for the many, many blessings. I am very happy that my book has been published. I put my trust in God and God never fails. Hopefully, you will enjoy reading this book and place it on a shelf inside your heart. When the cold winds of life beat at your door, reach for...

EXPRESSIONS FROM WITHIN

Wilbur T. Cole

Before we begin...

Pray

Allow God's spirit to engulf us with peace, love, and wisdom. Believe He will meet our every need. This is not just a book of poetry. It's a personal message to you from the God in me. My hope for us, through my words, through His words, passionately strengthen, our walk with Christ. Preemptively prick our hearts. Spiritually my desire is reception and conviction. Savor these words and keep them close. Remember, you 're not so bad.
Remember, we can be saved.

Note: If led by the spirit, please feel free to add more scripture reinforcing your faith.

TABLE OF CONTENTS

Spiritual

v

Inspirational

For clarity use King James Reference Bible

Spiritual

Lord Speak

Oh Lord

Speak to me

Let not my heart be troubled

The enemy comes to destroy my peace

Oh Lord

Speak to me

Even when the sun goes down

And the door closes behind me

Send your marvelous light

Oh Lord

Speak to me

Even when my burdens outweigh my fears and

After you've spoken

Place your Word

Inside my heart

Lord, give me the courage to share it

With your people

John 10:10. *The thief cometh not, but for the steal, and to kill, and to destroy: I am come that they might have life, and that they might have it more abundantly.*

Psalms 23. *The LORD is my shepherd; I shall not want. He maketh me to lie down in green pastures: he leadeth me beside the still waters. He restoreth my soul. he leadeth me in the paths of righteousness for his name's sake. Yea, though I walk through the valley of the shadow of death, I will fear no evil: for thou art with me- thy rod and they staff they comfort me. Thou preparest a table before me in the presence of mine enemies: thou anointest my head with oil my cup runneth over. Surely goodness and mercy shall follow me all the days of my life: and I will dwell in the house of the LORD for ever.*

_____

_____

_____

Rays

Rays of light illuminate

From the love of God

Rays of hope comfort us

Before the worst storm

Rays of joy are the rewards

For our conversion to

Christianity

II Corinthians 1:2-4. *Grace be to you and peace from God our Father, and from the Lord Jesus Christ. Blessed be God, even the Father of our Lord Jesus Christ, the Father of mercies, and the God of all comfort; Who comforteth us in all our tribulation, that we may be able to comfort them which are in any trouble, by the comfort wherewith we ourselves are comforted of God.*

Matthew 18:3. *And said, Verily I say unto you, except ye be converted, and become as little children, ye shall not enter into the kingdom of heaven.*

_____

_____

_____

Woven To Serve

Soft, warm and woven

Some people are like a fray

Hanging from clothing

Waiting to be burned

Snagged or plucked away

From the very thing that

Gave you life

Weaving a strong foundation

In Christ Jesus

Is our goal

So keep the lines tight

Maybe then you'll stay

INTACT

II Corinthians 5:1. *For we know that if our earthly house of this tabernacle were dissolved, we have a building of God, an house not made with hands, eternal in the heavens.*

II Timothy 2:19. *Nevertheless the foundation of God standeth sure, having this seal, The Lord Knoweth them that are his. And, Let every one that nameth the name of Christ depart from iniquity.*

Heaven

Success is a place you can choose

Where you want to go

Don't fall prey to your fears

Forgiveness is the vehicle to reach

Distant lands

I choose Heaven

The place God

Prepared for me

We're in Bondage to sin

Until we choose Him

Reconcile your Fate of Unforgiveness

I choose God

But He Chose Me First

Romans 8:15-17. *For ye have not received the spirit of bondage again to fear; but ye have received the Spirit of adoption, whereby we cry Abba, Father. The Spirit itself beareth witness with out spirit, that we are the children of God: And if children, then heirs; heirs of God, and joint-heirs with Christ; if so be that we suffer with him, that we may be also glorified together.*

Ephesians 1:3-4. *Blessed be the God and Father of our Lord Jesus Christ, who hath blessed us with all spiritual blessings in heavenly places in Christ: According as he hath chosen us in him before the foundation of the world, that we should be holy and without blame before him in love.*

_____

_____

_____

_____

_____

_____

Almost

I give salutations to the Creator

Who transformed me from

Condescending rags to glorified riches

I almost didn't make it

For mother's prayers which elevate me

Through hard times

I almost didn't make it

For the times in my life

When I made wrong turns

Only to be redirected by the Savior

I almost didn't make it

For the fathers that stand in the rain

Watching their sons

Day and night

Wither thy go

Had I listened to the enemy

The answer wouldn't

Be almost

Romans 12:2-3. *And be not conformed to this world: but be ye transformed by the renewing of your mind, that ye may prove what is that good, and acceptable, and perfect, will of God. For I say, through the grace given unto me, to every man that is among you, not to think of himself more highly than be ought to think; but to think soberly, according as God hath dealt to every man the measure of faith.*

Proverbs 3:5-6. *Trust in the LORD with all thine heart; and lean not unto thine own understanding In all thy ways acknowledge him, and he shall direct thy path.*

_____

_____

_____

Unexpected Grace

Agitation and Abrasive temperament

Disturb peace

Doc Meds control patients

By calming their fears

Your agenda is

Unimportant to God

Your bark is worst than your bite

If it scares

Loved ones away

The favor of God is a reward

For those with a

Discerning spirit

You labor in vain if your

Destiny is accompanied

By loneliness

Unexpected grace is still given

To solidify His

Love for us

Luke2:52. *And Jesus increased in wisdom and stature, and in favour with God and man.*

Ephesians 2:4-5. *But God, who is rich in mercy, for his great love wherewith he loved us, Even when we were dead in sins, hath quickened us together with Christ, (by grace ye are saved.)*

Beyond The Veil

Stonewall, Stone Cold

My heart calloused

By sin and shame

The door, the truth, and the life

Remove the blinders

From my eyes

I was wrong

The veil connects

My salvation to God

He gave His life on Calvary

His cleansing Blood

Removes earth's captivity

The veil has been

torn for me

Foundation has been

Laid for me

Matthew 27:51. *And, be hold, the veil of the temple was rent in twain from the top to the bottom; and the earth did quake, and the rocks rent.*

Psalm 104:5. *Who laid the foundation of the earth, that it should not be removed for ever.*

_____

_____

_____

The Trinity

The Peace of God

Gives me the

Strength to go on

Jesus gives me water

To drink so when I'm

Thirsty Jesus is my

Supplier, He's my Anchor

Sweet, sweet spirit

Comforts me

Before the worst storm

Eyes have not seen

Ears have not heard

The place God prepared

For me

Woven together, fortifies me

Before the fall

John 14:26-27. *But the Comforter, which is the Holy Ghost, whom the Father will send in my name, he shall teach you all things, and bring all things to your remembrance, whatsoever I have said unto you. Peace I leave with you, my peace I give unto you: not as the world giveth, give I unto you. Let not your heart be troubled, neither let it be afraid.*

Philippians 4:13. *I can do all things through Christ which strengtheneth me.*

_____

_____

_____

The Peace

The peace of God

Stills my Heart

After elevated snares

Darken my path

Grace congealed

Lay my pathway straight

Rewarded by golden

Stairs that lead to the Father

Pieces of a dream not

Perceivable by man

Stops the pain of dogmatic truths

The Peace of God

Stills my mind

After therapeutic Failure

Darkens my path

Pieces of nylon woven together

Give the trapeze artist peace

Knowing the net is there

To catch his fall

Proverbs 3:25-26. *Be not afraid of sudden fear, neither of the desolation of the wicked, when it cometh. For the LORD shall be thy confidence, and shall keep thy foot from being taken.*

Luke 1:79. *To give light to them that sit in darkness and in the shadow of death, to guide our feet into the way of peace.*

Psalms 34:14-16. *Depart from evil, and do good; seek peace, and pursue it. The eyes of the LORD are open unto their cry. The face of the LORD is against them that do evil, to cut off the remembrance of them from the earth.*

_____

_____

_____

Your Faithfulness

Tranquil moods

Are mediated for me

Solace stairs

Elevate my faith in Jesus

Metaphorically, I

Parenthetically phrase

(He's a Rock in a weary land)

(He's the Bright Morning Star)

(He's the Balm of Gilead)

That is healing in the valley

You've been freed from

Your infirmities

Fret not if you saw

The sun rise this morn

Your faith will activate

His Love

Proverbs 3:25-26. *Be not afraid of sudden fear, neither of the desolation of the wicked, when it cometh. For the LORD shall be thy confidence, and shall keep thy foot from being taken.*

Luke 1:79. *To give light to them that sit in darkness and in the shadow of death, to guide our feet into the way of peace.*

Psalms 34:14-16. *Depart from evil, and do good; seek peace, and pursue it. The eyes of the LORD are open unto their cry. The face of the LORD is against them that do evil, to cut off the remembrance of them from the earth.*

I Timothy 2:5. *For there is one God, and one mediator between God and men, the man Christ Jesus.*

_____
_____
_____

The Blood

Emollients are placated

By the love of God

The enemy is a liar

Generational curses can

Be broken...

The blood of Jesus covers

All iniquities

Teen pregnancy

Drug dealing

Alcoholism

Broken homes and divorce

Will be blotted out

By the blood of Jesus

Fall on your knees...

Fall on your knees and stay there

Until you receive God's perfect will

For your life

Ezekiel 36:26-27. *A new heart also will I give you, and a new spirit will I put within you: and I will take away the stony heart out of your flesh, and I will give you an heart of flesh. And I will put my spirit within you, and cause you to walk in my statutes, and ye shall keep my judgments, and do them.*

_____

_____

_____

Deliverance

Are your papers in order?
Real credence manifests itself
Based on facts
He called us with a Holy calling
Angelic voices are sent
To prevent future dangers
God wrote your orders before
The beginning of time
Have you lost your way?
Prophecy says a child will be born
If we receive him
He will lead us from destruction
Are we seeking deliverance?
From earth captivity,
Deliverance from idolatry
Deliverance from pleasure seeking flesh
The steps of a good man
Are ordered by God

Isaiah 9:6. *For unto us a child is born, unto us a son is given: and the government shall be upon his shoulder: and his name shall be call Wonderful, Counselor, The mighty God, The everlasting Father, The Prince of Peace.*

II Timothy 4:8. *Henceforth there is laid up for me a crown of righteousness, which the Lord, the righteous judge, shall give meat that day: and not to me only, but unto all them also that love his appearing.*

_____

_____

_____

Tagged By God

Livers and Hearts

They all must expire

Doc said

In your case

You're beyond repair

Even when man says

He has done all he can do

And the toe taggers

Come out to expedite your bad news

In the midst of storm

That places you at Heaven's door

One mistake man makes

Is not knowing he's

Been Tagged by God

Which gives Him, The last word

P.S. Thank you Lord, for saving my friend

Psalms 103:3-4. *Who forgiveth all thine iniquities; who healeth all thy diseases.*

Matthews 19:26. *But Jesus beheld them, and said unto them, With men this is impossible, but with God all things are possible.*

_____

_____

_____

Validated Ministry

A car is recognized by its sounds

And looks, four wheels

The rev of its engine

You were shaped and molded

In the image of God

How can you be a car

But sound like a train?

Train your mind not to yield

To temptation

A purpose driven life is gyrated

By the pistons of God

Your direction should be well mapped out and

Your mission should be well lubricated

With the Word

Never squeaky or sounding like tinkling brass

Be What God Created

You to Be

Acts 6:4. *But we will give ourselves continually to prayer, and to the ministry of the word.*

Proverbs 3:6. *In all thy ways acknowledge him, and he shall direct thy paths.*

Genesis 1:26. *And God said, Let us make man in our image, after our likeness: and Let them have dominion over the fish of the sea, and over the fowl of the air, and over the cattle, and over all the earth, and over every creeping thing that creepeth upon the earth.*

Timothy 2:7-8. *Whereunto I am ordained a preacher, and an apostle, (I speak the truth in Christ, and lie not); a teacher of the Gentiles in faith and verity. I will therefore that men pray every where, lifting up holy hands, without wrath and doubting.*

Psalms 25:19-20. *Consider mine enemies; for they are many; and they hate me with cruel hatred. 0 keep my soul, and deliver me: let me not be ashamed; for I put my trust in thee.*

_____

_____

_____

Show Me the Way

Lord, give me a new song
Lord, encourage my soul
Lord, give me a clean heart
Lord, dry my tears
Lord, restore the love in my home
Lord, quiet my fears
Lord, give me a new walk
Cause Lord I want to live for Thee
Lord, I know you didn't come to this
Place to live
Lord, I know you came to save my soul
You came to make me whole
You came to show me the way
Lord, give me a New Song
Lord, change my life completely
Lord, give me a new start
'Cause now, Lord, I want to live for Thee
Lord, I will never turn from you with
All my footsteps
Guided by Thee
Lord, give me a New Song
Lord, show me the way
29

Matthew 7:21. *Not every one that saith unto me, Lord, Lord, shall enter into the kingdom of heaven; but he that doeth the will of my Father which is in heaven.*

I Timothy 1:15-16. *This is a faithful saying, and worthy of all acceptation, that Christ Jesus came into the world to save sinners; of whom I am chief. Howbeit for this cause I obtained mercy, that in me first Jesus Christ might show forth all longsuffering, for a pattern to them which should hereafter believe on him to life everlasting.*

Psalms 25:4-5. *Show me thy ways, O Lord; teach me thy paths. Lead me in thy truth, and teach me: for thou art the God of my salvation; on thee do I wait all the day.*

_____

_____

_____

Hyperbole

Phylacteries used to

Keep your focus on

God, not hyperbole

The acceptance of all

Humanities is incomprehensible

Christians should continue

Being the salt of the earth

Not the cream

Don't worry who goes with

You when the Lord

Forbears your walk

Don't worry about clothes

Don't worry about food or drink

Didn't He care for the sparrow?

Which neither works nor produces manna?

The ultimate goal is to lead

Lost souls to Christ

Matthew 5:13. *Ye are the salt of the earth: but if the salt have lost his savour, wherewith shall it be salted? It is thenceforth good for nothing, but to be cast out, and to be trodden under foot of men.*

_____

_____

_____

Luxury of Peace

The peace of God

Gives our family

The peace to survive

If God is Peace

And if cleanliness is next

To Godliness

Cleanliness shouldn't

Destroy our peace

Pray that God gives us

The ability to clean and maintain

Our peace

God is not pleased

If things, places and attitudes

Destroy our peace

Attitude determines our altitude

Peace, Love and Heaven

Should be our goal

Numbers 6:26-27. *The LORD lift up his countenance upon thee, and give thee peace. And they shall put my name upon the children of Israel; and I will bless them.*

Can You Believe What God Has Done For Me?

Even when these old

Dry bones quake

And my Heart Beats

At an unfamiliar pace

God's Grace is sufficient for me

Even when a perfect

Storm erupts on a sunny day

It's no Match for a resurrected Christ

Who instills power in me

To combat any fight

It was God's Grace

Can you believe what God has done for me?

It was God's Grace

Can you believe what God has done for me?

He leadeth me beside the still waters

Can you believe what God has done for me?

It was nothing I did on my own

Can you believe what God has done for me?

It wasn't because I've been so good

It was God's Grace

Believe It

Psalm 23:2. *He maketh me to lie down in green pastures: he leadeth me in the paths of righteousness for his name's sake.*

Job 4:14. *Fear came upon me and trembling which made all my bones shake.*

Do You Really Love The Lord?

Do you really love the Lord
Like you say you Love the Lord?
Can you do His will when the
Way is Dark?
Do you really have Faith
Like you say you have faith?
Can you step out on nothing
And find a blessing in place?
Do you really trust the Lord
Like you say you Trust?
Have you been tried by the fire,
Have you been washed in his Blood?
You know I really Love the Lord
Like I say I love the Lord
I really Love the Lord
Because He first loved me
He gave His life when He went to Calvary
But know it's us who are too blind to see:
For it 's easy to say I really Love the Lord
But how many of us can follow His word?

II Corinthians 4:8. *We are troubled on every side, yet not distressed; we are perplexed, but not in despair.*

_____

_____
_____

_____

It's Already Done

Child by child, a glimmer of light
Rays shining in my soul
The sparrow wants not, he's in God's Love
Don't worry now
It's Already Done
The clouds hang low but His spirit reigns high
Don't worry now
It's Already Done
The pain flows through my tortured body
Seeking to capture my soul but I press on, I press on
Because He made a promise to me,
He made a promise to you
Don't worry now
It's Already Done
Don't feel discouraged, don't feel dismayed
He'll help me through my hard times
He'll put food on my table
He's a way out of no way, He's Alpha and Omega
That's the Beginning and the End
It's already done
It's already done
Storm clouds are passing through
Don't worry now

It's already done.

He'll restore strength to my body

He's water when I'm thirsty

He's bread when I'm Hungry, so don't worry now

It's Already Done

Luke 12:23-24. *The life is more than meat, and the body is more than raiment. Consider the ravens: for they neither sow nor reap; which neither have storehouse nor barn; and God feedeth them: how much more are ye better than the fowls?*

Revelation 1:8. *I am Alpha and Omega, the beginning and the ending, saith the Lord, which is, and which was, and which is to come, the Almighty.*

_____

_____

_____

I'm Anxious

I'm anxious to see the King
I will not trust in my bow
Neither shall my sword save me
God will put down thy enemy's hand
And anyone who treads against thee
God judges the righteous
God is angry with the wicked every day
If he turn not he will whet His sword
He hath bent his bow against persecutors
That's why I should allow the Lord to fight my battles
No weapon formed against me shall prosper
The sword of the spirit teaches me to
Love my enemies
And bless them that curse me
Pray for them that despitefully use me
Bows and arrows can't save me
I need the word of God
It will comfort me
It will protect me in the time of storm
Don't be anxious to achieve worldliness
My treasures are stored in heaven

Psalms 44:6-7. *For I will not trust in my bow, neither shall my sword save me. But thou hast saved us from our enemies, and hast put them to shame that hated us.*

_____

_____

_____

Provision

My father's unimpeded process
Of watching and
Working out my problems
In ways incomprehensible to me
Not getting what I
Wanted, but supplying
My every need
My shelter while
The tempests rage
My food when the ground is
Stone cold
Even when I refused to go
He allowed a big fish
To consume me, and transport
Me, where He wanted
And placed my feet on solid ground
He will provide

Philippians 4:19. *But my God shall supply all your needs according to his riches in glory by Christ Jesus.*

_____

_____

_____

Transparency

Maturity allows you to face
Your weaknesses
Embarrassment is secondary
To the Revelations of
Truth
Rudimentarily admitting
Your faults is the
Beginning of wisdom
Hiding your mistakes
Retards correction
A labyrinth
Is a maze of unforgiveness
Break the chains of bondage
By confessing and
Testifying God's Goodness
Tell us how He
Brought you through
If I can see your heart
Then I know
Who you are

II Corinthians 12:9. *And he said unto me, My grace is sufficient for thee: for my strength is made perfect in weakness. Most gladly therefore will I rather glory in my infirmities, that the power of Christ may rest upon me.*

Faith

Misalignment causes irreconcilable differences

Stemming from being unbalanced

Infidelity arrives when you marry

An unbeliever pretending to be a Christian

To align your lives in Christ requires

FAITH

II Corinthians 6:14. *Be ye not unequally yoked together with unbelievers: for what fellowship hath righteousness with unrighteousness? And what communion hath light with darkness?*

Matthew 7:21. *Not every one that saith unto me, Lord, Lord, shall enter into the kingdom of heaven; but he that doeth the will of my Father which is in heaven.*

In Touch

Life is not fair

Being in touch with God develops a shield of

Protection that encircles us

Despite the travesty

He's in touch with our destiny

Ephesians 6:11. *Put on the whole armour of God, that ye may be able to stand against the wiles of the devil.*

_____

_____

_____

The Ultimate Gift

A perfect gift is ordained by God

Receive it with HUMILITY and

Cherish it with Love

Ephesians 3:17. *That Christ may dwell in your hearts by faith; that ye, being rooted and grounded in love.*

Jesus' Death

Jesus' death on the cross
Is the epiphany for all our sins?
The possibility to recover just
One of those transgressions is irretrievable
All that are saved were in the tree of life
Before the beginning of time
That is a reasonable assessment
Of true sanctification

Isaiah 53:5-6. *But he was wounded for our transgressions; he was bruised for our iniquities: the chastisement of our peace was upon him; and with his stripes we are healed. All we like sheep have gone astray; we have turned every one to his own way; and the LORD hath laid on him the iniquity of us all.*

_____

_____

_____

Inspirational

Master Refurbish

Master, refurbish regency in me

Exercising the ruling power of the majority

My back is weak and my vision is going dim

Why can't my people make amends?

Lift thy head to look straight ahead

Patches for my knees for a long fervent prayer

If thou bow down

Only for a moment

Make sure my heart

Never forgets the struggle

Psalm 16:8-11. *I have set the LORD always before me: because he is at my right hand, I shall not be moved. Therefore my heart is glad, and my glory rejoiceth: my flesh also shall rest in hope. For thou wilt not leave my soul in hell; neither wilt thou suffer thine Holy One to see corruption. Thou wilt show me the path of life: in thy presence is fullness of joy; at thy right hand there are pleasures for evermore.*

_____

_____

_____

Peace

Peace

Is a sign moving in

The right direction!

Forced peace

Is a waste of time!

Inner peace

Is the cure of the world today?

Isaiah 26:3. *Thou wilt keep him in perfect peace, whose mind is stayed on thee: because he trusted in thee.*

Father

If thy earthly

father sins,

Don't despair

God will deliver you

From your worst nightmare.

53

Chastity and Purity

Chastity and purity
A long, lost art is overridden
By the aggressive vigor
Of a male counterpart
To restore morality in
Our sons and daughters
We need a miracle
And some mercy from
The only begotten Son

Sin A' Comin'

If you sense sin a' comin'
Just keep a runnin'
You'll find happiness there
If you sense sin a comin'
Don't walk, keep runnin'
Sin will soon despair

Liberalism

Political correctness is a man made
Term designed to circumvent
Us down unyielding roads
Engulfing our soul with the
Perversions of this world
Understanding our Heavenly
Father's salvation will create
A far better reward

More Or Less

We need to act more

Procrastinate less

We need to give more

Find fault less

We need to pray more

Sin less

Realize that thinking secular

Makes you MORAL LESS!!!

Cheesecake and Apple Strudel

Cheesecake and apple strudel

Will expand your waistline

School and work will make a man

Sin and pleasure a synonymous pair

Love and honor will get you there

Matthew 6:25-26. *Therefore I say unto you, Take no thought for you life, what ye shall eat, or what ye shall drink; nor yet for your body, what ye shall put on. Is not the We more than meat, and the body than raiment? Behold thy sow not, neither do they reap, nor gather into barns; yet your heavenly Father feedeth them. Are ye not much better than they?*

Peace and Harmony

Peace and harmony will help race relations
After pain and grit come emancipation
To forgive and forget will ensure a cure
For animosity
Seize your freedom
To avoid stagnation

_____

Success

A key to success is a chance
At life
You made it; I made it
Because our parents had
Virtue,
Conformity of life
Don't destroy an innocent
Life
Before it has a chance for success

Decency

Decency, Good Taste and Modesty
Recognizable attributes of morality
Concerns with family quality
There must be a concentrated
Effort to avoid promiscuity
A discipline that controls annuity
A systematic approach to show daily support
Of the weakness of the flesh
Without cruelty
Satisfaction comes from knowing your mate
Excitement anticipating your sweetness
Everyday!!!!!!!!

Titus 2:11-12. *For the grace of God that bringeth salvation hath appeared to all men, Teaching us that, denying ungodliness and worldly lusts, we should live soberly, righteously, and godly, in this present world.*

_____
_____
_____

Steel Gray Magnolias

Steel gray magnolias
Love on the horizon
Our eyes meet with a
Surprising interest
No fog today
The stillness of
A silent breath of life
In our direction, fire and ice
A sweet mixture of love

Escaping

Evasion only delays
The confrontation of the altercation
Escaping only gives
Temporary peace
The secular world
Looks forward to the future
Morals are missing in action
Decency falls behind
As for me
Faith is my stronghold

My Heart Aches

My heart aches

When I see my brother cry,

He has a habit

He cannot escape

His fervent prayer

Is to be normal and

Balanced, you see...

A smart man sets goals,

Makes plans, and nourishes his family

But he has a habit

He cannot escape

I Corinthians 10:13. *There hath no temptation taken you but such as is common to man: but God is faithful, who will not suffer you to be tempted above that ye are able; but will with the temptation also make a way to escape, that ye may be able to bear it.*

I Kings 5:9. *My servants shall bring them down from Lebanon unto the sea: and I will convey them by sea in floats unto the place that thou shalt appoint me, and will cause them to be discharged there, and thou shalt receive them: and thou shalt accomplish my desire, in giving food for my household.*

Slavery Is a Labyrinth

Slavery is a labyrinth

Locked there in

A never ending maze

Of discrimination, even my friend's

Why is the hatred not forgotten?

Over many years

They have the advantage

Yet, they still fear

Blood and sweat from our ancestors' brow

Often extend my

Freedom without a plow

Equality is a dream not perceivable by man

Hatred for nothing...

Yet life is still grand

Work

Work is to wealth as

Laziness is to starvation

To control a horse

Requires a harness and a bit

To control some people

Requires a jail cell...

Why can't we learn from the past?

II Thessalonians 3: 7-10. *For yourselves know how ye ought to follow us: for we behaved not ourselves disorderly among you; Neither did we eat any man's bread for nought; but wrought with labour and travail night and day, that we might not be chargeable to any of you: Not because we have not power, but to make ourselves an example unto you to follow us. For even when we were with you, this we commanded you, that if any would not work, neither should he eat.*

_____

_____

_____

Crack Cocaine

I saw a bird land
On a utility wire
One hundred feet in the air
The bird began to strike
The hazardous surface of
the wire to no avail.
The voltage was protected
By the outer layers .
However, with repeated strikes
The bird finally penetrated the
Wire and got fried.
Save yourself.
Get off the wire.

To Be or Not To Be

To be or not to be

That is the question

You had a chance at life

But it slipped through your possession

If the grass is greener on the other side

Why do I use white snow

Which causes me to subside?

Remember God's strength

Or feel His wrath

He's capable of removing worldly pleasures

From your current path

I Corinthians 6:19-20. *What? Know ye not that your body is the temple of the Holy Ghost which is in you, which ye have of God, and ye are not your own? For ye are bought with a price: therefore glorify God in your body, and in your spirit, which are God's.*

Matthew 6:23-24. *But if thine eye be evil, thy whole body shall be full of darkness. If therefore the light that is in thee be darkness, how great is that darkness! "No man can serve two masters: for either he will hate the one, and love the other; or else he will hold to the one, and despise the other. Ye cannot serve God and mammon.*

Success Is the Reward

Success is the reward

For persistence

Humbleness in a senior citizen

Is from the love of God

Morality considerably are the rewards

For avoidance of promiscuity

Paul and Silas

Illuminate hope

For prisoners in dark, unforgivable cells

Psalm 127:3-5. *Lo, children are a heritage of the LORD and the fruit of the womb is his reward. As arrows are in the hand of a mighty man; so are children of the youth. Happy is the man that hath his quiver full of them: they shall not be ashamed, but they shall speak with the enemies in the gate.*

I Corinthians 6:9-10. *Know ye not that the unrighteous shall not inherit the kingdom of God? Be not deceived: neither fornicators, nor idolaters, nor adulterers, nor effeminate, nor abusers of them selves with mankind, nor thieves, nor covetous, nor drunkards, nor revilers, nor extortioners, shall inherit the kingdom of God.*

_____

_____

_____

My Stomach Is Full

My stomach is full
My purse is fat
I drive the best cars
At my house I just relax
My boss is fair
My mind is full of happy things
--Except Rejection--
Which always draws near?

Eternal Comfort

A blade of grass withers and passes away,
A storm darkens my path
Infinite tears flood my soul
Through the years I keep on toiling
Loved ones struggle to press on
After twilight called you home
Peace in the midst of confusion
Trying to understand that which
Makes the green grass green
Drop your anchor in the Port of the Lord
And ye shall receive Blessings unspeakable
Going on with the ability God gave me
Seen clearly after scales fall from my eyes
(Selah), God's passion replenishes years lost
With all power in His hands
God's Grace and Mercy dried my tears
And restored my soul
Servant, well done

_____
_____
_____

Infested

Infested with fleas, mites, and parasites
We're a proud people
Death before dishonor
The government pushed me and
Prodded me like cattle or sheep
Go west, my son ,here you are too near to me.
"Get A Little Farther, You Are Too Near To Me"
I searched the forest for an Indian
Today, a tomahawk, a teepee and even maize
Jew man, Black man don't feel dismay
The government implemented genocide
Stole land away and traded buffalo
The modern way
Our women raped, our heads scalped
We hung from the gallows for protecting our rights
Neither holocaust nor slavery wiped out
A race of people, it mercilessly removed numbers
From the ranks

A proud people that fertilized, the land,

Body and soul

Signed treaty after treaty, only to be broken

To obtain more land.

Matthew 6:14-15. *For if ye forgive men their trespasses, your heavenly Father will also forgive you. But if ye forgive not men their trespasses, neither will your Father forgive your trespasses.*

_____

_____

_____

Crown of Gold

Feathers for my crown
Now I wear a frown
Since the big ships rolled in
Fields of maize
Little papoose
Scampering in the distance
Feathers for my crown
I gave furs
I gave land
Now I have a crown of gold and
Only the buffalo to help me stand
If you listen closely
My voice is trapped
Between the whippoorwill and the robin
Feathers for my crown
With blood stained tears
Now I wear a crown of gold

James 1:11-12. *For the sun is no sooner risen with a burning heat, but it withereth the grass, and the flower thereof falleth, and the grace of the fashion of it perisheth: so also shall the rich man fade away in his ways. Blessed is the man that endureth temptation: for when he is tried, he shall receive the crown of life, which the Lord hath promised to them that love him.*

New Orleans

Diversity curves inequality

Modesty curves profanity

Love instills Christianity

Sin is companion with immorality

Acceptance is an attack of lunacy

When the world is crumbling at your feet

Focus your attention on

Respect and decency

When it is your turn at bat

We can rebuild

However, we should

Learn from the past

Proverbs 15:3-4. *The eyes of the LORD are in every place, beholding the evil and the good. A wholesome tongue is a tree of life: but perverseness therein is a breach in the spirit.*

Interracial Marriage

Interracial marriages are not preferred
By choice
Considerably, they are like lightning bolts
Never striking twice in the same place
Consequently and inevitably they are like food
Spoilage is definite without proper care
Interracial marriages
Chances for survival increase with
Maturity and frugality
Chances of survival increase with
Love and understanding
Fidelity stuck with adhesiveness
When respect and empathy are common place
Peace and harmony are possible with any race
Holy matrimony is harmonious with
Any marriage joined by God
Success is possible until you
Fall in a stupor

Ideas

I have an idea

But since it's conjectural

It's rejected by the masses

Socially, morally, and congenially

It's better to keep

Your idea to yourself

A Sister's Love

A sister's love

Is felt from a distance

Despite the world

And the trouble therein

She excels for herself

And never looks back

Genuinely, she wants her brother

On the right track

She will never sacrifice her freedom

She is no fool

She will soothe your wounds

After a battle with the world

She is no fool...

A man must show his independence

Sister, Sister

Sister, sister

What is the reason

For our black faces?

We didn't come this far

To destroy each other

Where is the joy and love for thy brother?

Sister, sister

Why use a system you own not

While destroying your brother

With a stomach full of knots

Package of Love

Package of love

Inspiration of you

Void of vanity

Infallibly true

A matron in

Charge of her life

With God protecting

Her path

She's my woman

A complete package of love

Proverbs 3:17-18. *Her ways are way of pleasantness, and all her paths are peace. She is a tree of life to them that lay hold upon her: and happy is every one that retaineth her.*

We Found

My eyes form water at the

Thought of losing my spouse

Conjecturably, the judge separates

Legally the love we found

The test of time...

Sweet music to my ears

As for me

As for me

Love continues to endure

Jeremiah 31:1-3. *At the same time, saith the LORD, will I be the God of all the families of Israel, and they shall be my people. Thus saith the LORD, The people which were left of the sword found grace in the wilderness; even Israel, when I went to cause him to rest. The LORD hath appeared of old unto me, saying, Yea, I have loved thee with an everlasting love: therefore with loving kindness have I drawn thee.*

_____

_____

_____

Sweetness

Is your alias
Our thoughts of love combined
Eyes closed to capture inner beauty
'Cause life with you is divine
The warmth of your aura
The wind in your hair
Your sweetness is desired
Without flair
Chemistry is the thought of
Our bodies and mind
Your sweetness is my treat
'Cause life with you is divine

My Hometown

The Big M'town sweet 'que
Slow baked on a summer day
Calapari envisioned a Final Four
While West led Grizzlies, but lost
Pennies in search of a dynasty.
Al Barkay'd while Isaac brought
Funk to the River City.
Herenton led Peabody ducks down Beale
To create our own southern mecca.
Hood rats and ghetto rangers control the
Southside while crystal laden
Oriental rugs cover G'town.
Nude shakers bounce while Reverend Netters-
A.R.. Williams and Keith Norman strengthen
Our walk with Christ.
201 fills as gang bangers
deal dope to dopes.
Hard work, one lover, encapsulate
My love for this Big M'town.

Life in Memphis

Sifting through the rubble
After life's earthquake
Sitting in the court room
Palms sweaty, eyes giddy
Police brutality unnecessary pain
To my head
Drug deal gone bad
On the wrong side of the tracks
Shots fired
Women crying, babies famished
And left in the heat
Money preferred over education
My transmission leaking
My fan belt broke
Life in Memphis is unmistakably no joke

Dichotomyville

Where is Dichotomyville?

Surprisingly it could be your hometown

You see it lies between your left

Ear and your right ear

You see it lies between

The rich and the poor

It's not just conventional

Black and white

You see, it lies between your opinions

And mine - Dichotomyville

Your headlights should

Break the fog of gloom

By now you should realize that Dichotomyville

Is your hometown

The fork in the road

That could lead to destruction

The place where daylight falls and

Night glistens

Suppressed contradiction that

Opposes my idea

Dichotomyville ninny is here

Mo' Credible

Father create in me a clean heart
The son can only see the light
The Father illuminates
Don't fool yourself
A good name is better than riches
A credible son is received more
Often than a son, the Father
Allowed to slip through the
Cracks of life
Give your son your legacy before
The dust cries out for your soul
The ultimate responsibility of the
Father is to make the son
Mo' Credible

I'm Coming Home

I'm on my way home
I'm rounding the bend
I'm looking for a sign to come in
Yellow ribbon round an old oak tree
Soothe my heart
My Father is waiting with
A robe to put on me, and
A ring of gold to show the world
It's safe to come back
From the clutches of sin
He prepared the best meat
To celebrate my union
Now I have Jesus
And a psalm to carry me through
I'm coming home

Luke 15:20-24. *And he arose, and came to his father. But when he was yet a great way off, his father saw him, and had compassion, and ran, and fell on his neck, and kissed him. And the son said unto him, Father, I have sinned against heaven, and in thy sight, and am no more worthy to be called thy son. But the father said to his servants, Bring forth the best robe, and put it on him; and put a ring on his hand, and shoes on his feet: And bring hither the fatted calf and kill it; and let us eat, and be merry. For this my son was dead, and is alive again; he was lost, and is found. And they began to be merry.*

Wisdoms

Ever turn on a street only to find it to be a dead end? In life we find dead ends. If this happens to you, simply pick up your Bible and wait for Divine Guidance. OH YEAH!

Life gives us different forms of disappointments. Accepting them breaks the chain of our God given ability to fight on.

Finally realized a failed marriage is a intermission while GOD chisels ,cuts, breaks, and diminishes our selfish ways. Women, give your man reconciliation.

At night the sea is dark; a ship could drift endlessly. Then a beacon light emits from a LIGHTHOUSE sending a ray of HOPE. I'm coming HOME. JESUS IS THAT LIGHT!

While serving my Country, I was on a military operation off the coast of Cuba. The marine landing vehicle I was on stalled. It started sinking, but by God's grace "I'm Still Here"... God has a plan for you as well. Hold on to your faith.

About the Author...

Wilbur T Cole, a native Memphian, graduated from East High School in 1978, and enlisted in the US. Marines. After serving in the military from 1978-1982, he became a Corrections Officer at the Shelby County Correction Center in 1983. Mr. Cole started his U.S. Postal Service career in 1984 and is currently a Germantown Postman. W.T. is a member of First Baptist Broad under the anointed leadership of Pastor Keith Norman. As an author and poet, W.T. is forever grateful to family and friends for their support during his creative work.

To Order Additional Copies of

Expressions From Within

Go to:
www.expressionsbycole.com
wtcole@expressionsbycole.com

Or Contact:
WTC Publishing
PO Box 382011
Germantown, TN 38183

Special Rates Available
Wholesale to Retail

Order by Mail:
Send $15.00 + 5.00 S&H

$20.00 to

W. T. Cole
PO Box 382011
Germantown, TN 38183